Moral Purity

Charles R. Swindoll

Charles R. Swindoll is a graduate of Dallas Theological Seminary and has served in pastorates for over twenty-two years, including churches in Texas, New England, and California. Since 1971 he has served as senior pastor of the First Evangelical Free Church of Fullerton, California. Chuck's radio program, "Insight for Living," began in 1979. In addition to his church and radio ministries, Chuck has authored twenty books and numerous booklets on a variety of subjects.

Publisher:	Insight for Living, Fullerton, California
Creative Director:	Cynthia Swindoll
Editorial Assistants:	Jane Gillis, Wendy Jones, and Karene Wells
Communications Manager:	Carla Beck
Production Supervisor:	Deedee Snyder
Production Assistant:	Linda Robertson
Designer:	Michael Standlee Design
Production Artists:	Trina Crockett and Rhonda DiBello
Printer:	Penn Lithographics, Inc.
Typographer:	Trina Crockett
Calligraphers:	Graphique Design Studio and Carla Randolph
Cover:	Painting by D. Ridgway Knight, *At the Well,* © 1983 Haddad's Fine Arts, Inc., The Brooklyn Museum, Brooklyn, Gift of Mr. and Mrs. William E. S. Griswold

First printing 1985
Printed in the United States of America

ISBN 0-88070-135-8

I am well aware of the numerous written materials available today on the subject of moral purity. But I am even *more* aware of the enormous propaganda to which we are all exposed. Our minds and our emotions are easily lured off target by what I often call "the system." By that I mean the endless, relentless bombardment from the world in which we live. Its messages are subtle and bold, written and spoken, always attractive, remarkably convincing, and clever indeed.

Realizing the effectiveness of this sensual network, I am of the opinion that there needs to be a continual stream of information made available to the public that counteracts this force, presenting scriptural truth in an equally convincing manner. Erroneous thinking that leads to evil actions needs to be confronted. Because "the system" operates twenty-four hours a day, seven days every week, it is doubtful that Christians have come anywhere near overstating their position. With determination and diligence we must continue to make known a perspective that exposes "the system" and penetrates the moral fog which envelopes all who live on this planet. New materials must be put into print if for no other reason than to make a strong, relevant statement on behalf of godliness, purity, and truth; hence, this booklet.

Although brief, it is forthright. Other works may be more thorough, but none are written with greater passion or deeper conviction. As a pastor since the early 1960s, I have observed a tragic decline—a lowering of the standard of moral excellence—even within Christian circles. What was once confined to "the system" has now invaded the Church. That fact alone is enough to justify an increase in our effort to publish materials that both uphold the need for personal holiness and declare the consequences of an immoral lifestyle.

If something I have written helps you to walk away from wrong that has held you in bondage and draws you back to the truth that will set you free, the purpose of this booklet will have been achieved.

Chuck Swindoll
Fullerton, California

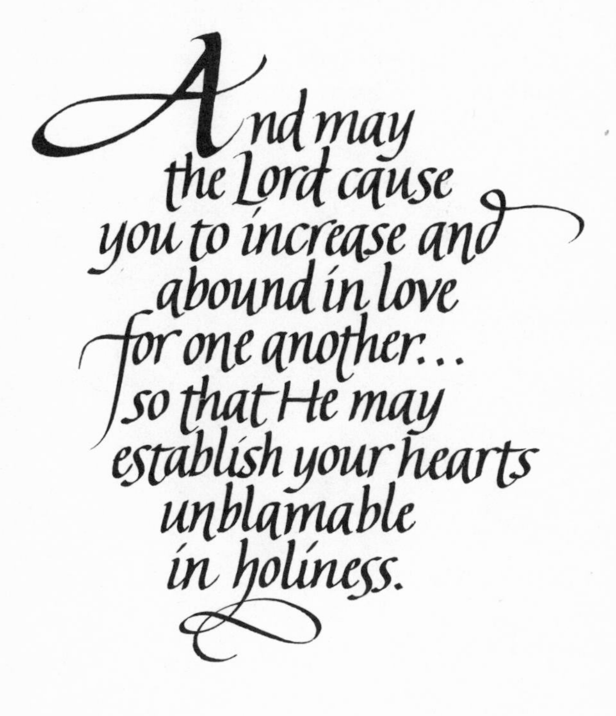

I THESSALONIANS 3:12–13a

Moral Purity

Holiness sounds scary. It need not be, but to the average American it is. Our tendency is to think that holiness would never find its way into a salesperson's office; certainly not that of an aggressive and successful athletic coach. Nor would a mother of small children be that concerned about holiness, or a teenager involved in a busy high school; to say nothing of some collegian pursuing a career with his or her eyes on great financial goals. Let's face it, holiness is something for the cloistered halls of a monastery. It needs organ music, long prayers, and religious-sounding chants. It hardly seems appropriate for those in the real world of the twentieth century. Author John White seems to agree with that.

> Have you ever gone fishing in a polluted river and hauled out an old shoe, a tea kettle or a rusty can? I get a similar sort of catch if I cast as a bait the word *holiness* into the murky depths of my mind. To my dismay I come up with such

associations as:

thinness
hollow-eyed gauntness
beards
sandals
long robes
stone cells
no sex
no jokes
hair shirts
frequent cold baths
fasting
hours of prayer
wild rocky deserts
getting up at 4 A.M.
clean fingernails
stained glass
self-humiliation[1]

Is that the mental picture you have when you think of holiness? Most do. It's almost as though holiness is the private preserve of an austere group of monks, missionaries, mystics, and martyrs. But nothing could be further from the truth.

As a matter of fact, holiness *does* belong in the life of the teenager. Holiness *does* have a place in the office of the salesperson. It is, indeed, appropriate in the world of the up-to-date, aggressive, even successful individual.

I couldn't be in greater agreement with Chuck Colson's statement: "Holiness is the everyday business of every Christian. It evidences itself in the decisions we make and the things we do, hour by hour, day by day."[2]

The Fog: An Analysis of Today's Moral Scene

Before going any further, let's back off a few feet and get a little perspective on the moral scene today. To penetrate the fog will take some effort, I can assure you. Perhaps it will help to read the writings of a sixth-century B.C. prophet named Habakkuk. His name looks like a misprint, doesn't it? On the contrary, the man was a bold voice for holiness in a day of compromise. A misfit, perhaps, but no misprint. Had you lived in his day, you may have wondered about his sanity! He was the kind of man who just wouldn't "get in line." His world was corrupt, but he believed in personal purity, of all things! How strange . . . yet how significant! We may not be familiar with him, but we surely understand his times.

He's a man who was surrounded by a moral fog. His book is an ancient call to repentance. It is a holy cry to God for divine intervention. And it's not just a cry; it's more like a scream. He says:

How long, O Lord, will I call for help,
And Thou wilt not hear?
I cry out to Thee, "Violence!"
Yet Thou dost not save. (Hab. 1:2)

He saw immoral and brutal acts of violence. So, of course, he asked, "Why?" He also asked, *"How long?"* He struggled with God's lack of immediate action. Though the prophet prayed, God seemed unusually distant. "How long? Why?" The heavens were brass. "Why don't You act decisively? Why don't You unfold Your arms and get with it in this old, polluted world of ours?

How long before You deliver Your people, Lord?" He continues:

Why dost Thou make me see iniquity,
And cause me to look on wickedness?
Yes, destruction and violence are
before me;
Strife exists and contention arises.
Therefore, the law is ignored
And justice is never upheld.
For the wicked surround the righteous;
Therefore, justice comes out
perverted. (vv. 3–4)
Art Thou not from everlasting,
O Lord, my God, my Holy One?
We will not die. (v. 12a)

"I thought You were holy. Aren't You the Holy One? Then how in the world can You sit back and do so little about my unholy world?" "[Habakkuk] could not reconcile a bad world with a holy God."[3]

How bad was his world? As we just observed, it was a world of brutal violence (v. 2) so severe that the prophet screamed out his prayer. It was a world of personal iniquity and wickedness (v. 3). *"Why dost Thou make me see* iniquity. . . ." The word includes "lying, vanity, and idolatry." "Why do You cause me to look on *wickedness*. . . ." That Hebrew term encompasses "oppression, robbery, and assault."

There were crimes of homicide going on in the streets. "Aren't You Jehovah of Judah? Aren't You the God of this nation? Where are You, God?"

There were strife and relational wrangling. There were arguments in homes, fights between parents and kids as well as between marital partners—not to mention wrangling between bosses and employees. And did you notice another relevant issue? The law was not being upheld. And when it was, it was being compromised. What a scene! It's going to sound familiar: brutal violence, personal iniquity, relational wrangling, legal compromise. You'd think Habakkuk lived in the inner city of some American metropolis.

I smiled when I was listening to a rather well-known Bible expositor several months ago. He said he'd just completed a serious study into the fourth, fifth, and sixth centuries B.C. and found himself intrigued to discover what they wrestled with back then.

He mentioned five issues that concerned those ancient people: (1) the eminent outbreak of international hostility; (2) the breakup of homes—weakening marriages; (3) the rebellion of youth and their lack of respect for parents or for the elderly; (4) the corruption in politics—integrity was undermined; and (5) the chug holes in the public roads!

Does that sound familiar? Does it sound like something you could identify with? History certainly has a way of repeating itself!

That's what makes Habakkuk's complaint so timely. "I thought You were holy, God! Where are You? How can You allow this to happen? I'm surrounded by a fog of moral pollution and I'm tired of breathing it in. I'm tired of its diseased impact on my life. I'm beginning to wonder about a holy God in a world of people *this* unholy." Maybe those are your sentiments, too.

Habakkuk cried aloud. Another prophet, named Jeremiah, just quietly sobbed. I have in mind his words as recorded in Jeremiah 6. He lived a little later than Habakkuk, though not by much. Habakkuk feared the nation's demise, but Jeremiah lived to see the nation destroyed.

That's why he wrote Lamentations, which is another name for *weeping.* Appropriately, Jeremiah is called *the weeping prophet.* He doesn't scream. He doesn't fight. He doesn't even argue. He just sobs. He writes his prophecy while wiping tears from his eyes.

"Be warned, O Jerusalem,
Lest I be alienated from you;
Lest I make you a desolation,
A land not inhabited." (Jer. 6:8)

Verse 10a:

To whom shall I speak and give warning,
That they may hear?
Behold, their ears are closed.

Understand, that's the result of living in the fog. "The system" takes its toll. Your ears slowly become closed, so much so that you can't hear the spiritual message God is giving. *"They cannot listen."* Observe the way he puts it:

The word of the Lord has become a reproach to them;
They have no delight in it. (v. 10b)

Do you want to know how that sounds in today's terms? "Aw, c'mon . . . get off that stuff! Get up with the times, man! All that prophet-of-doom talk is old hat. This is where it's at!" In Jeremiah's words, *"They have no delight in it"*—that is, in hearing the truth about holiness.

But I am full of the wrath of the Lord:
I am weary with holding it in. (v. 11a)

"I'm boiling. I'm churning . . . I'm so tired, Lord."

"For from the least of them even to the greatest of them,
Everyone is greedy for gain." (v. 13a)

Does that sound familiar?

Again, these verses describe life as it is lived in a moral fog. There is a constant fighting for gain. There's competition to get more and more. And to make matters worse:

"From the prophet even to the priest
Everyone deals falsely." (v. 13b)

Jeremiah weeps, "It's bad enough that it's in the law courts, but it's now in the pulpits, my Lord. It's to the place where I can't trust the one who wears a collar, who says he speaks for You. I can't be sure that those who are robed with the mantle of God tell me the truth anymore. They deal falsely. They have healed the wound of Your people just slightly." Look at what he says! "They keep saying, 'Shalom, shalom!' when there is no shalom! There isn't any peace. But they keep saying, 'Don't worry. Don't worry. It's gonna be okay,' when it's *not* going to be okay."

And if you don't think *that's* bad, look at verse 15.

"Were they ashamed because of the abomination they have done?
They were not even ashamed at all;
They did not even know how to blush."

Honestly now, did you know the Bible spoke of a time in history when people were so caught up in an immoral lifestyle that they no longer blushed? Jeremiah sobs, "I notice, God, that there are no more red faces. No one seems shocked anymore."

Today I suppose we could call it compensating or maybe rationalizing. In order to handle the shock of our day, we compensate by remaining free of shock. I repeat, that's part of living in the fog.

Psychiatrist Karl Menninger took up the pen of a prophet when he wrote *Whatever Became of Sin?* In that searching book he admits, "In a discussion of the sin of *lust* we have to allow for a considerable shift in the social code during the past century. It has been called a revolution, and perhaps it is. Many forms of sexual activity which for centuries were considered reprehensible, immoral, and sinful *anywhere,* and their public exhibition simply *anathema,* are now talked and written about and exhibited on the stage and screen."[4]

From *Honesty, Morality, and Conscience,* by Jerry White, I find a similar concern:

> We live in the age of freedom of expression and freedom of lifestyle. X-rated movies and magazines are available in every city. Legislation to control pornography has failed in most places. The sexual fiction of yesterday is the reality of today. Magazines displayed in supermarkets present articles featuring unmarried couples living together. Sex manuals advocate extramarital affairs. Fewer and fewer teenagers leave high school as virgins. Prime-time television flaunts homosexuality and infidelity.[5]

Pitirim Sorokin, formerly professor of sociology at Harvard, laments:

> There has been a growing preoccupation of our writers with the social sewers, the

broken homes of disloyal parents and unloved children, the bedroom of the prostitute, a cannery row brothel, a den of criminals, a ward of the insane, a club of dishonest politicians, a street corner gang of teenage delinquents, a hate-laden prison, a crime-ridden waterfront, the courtroom of a dishonest judge, the sex adventures of urbanized cavemen and rapists, the loves of adulterers and fornicators, of masochists, sadists, prostitutes, mistresses, playboys. Juicy loves, ids, orgasms, and libidos are seductively prepared and served with all the trimmings.[6]

And to add Jeremiah's observation: Nobody blushes anymore. It's all part of the moral pollution . . . the fog. "The system" may be insidious, but it is effective.

In every major city today, with a turn of the television dial, you can bring explicit sex right into your home for anybody to watch. And nobody blushes.

You don't even have to go into an "adult" bookstore anymore to find pornography. You can find it in quick-stop grocery stores or in some large drugstores and supermarkets. You may have to look a little, but it's there. Again I remind you, nobody blushes.

The ultimate, telltale sign of a low view of personal holiness is that we no longer blush when we find wrong. Instead, we make jokes about it. We re-dress immorality and make it appear funny. And if you don't laugh, you're considered a prude . . . you're weird . . . you're kind of crotchety.

Maybe I don't like to laugh about that anymore because as a minister I am forced to deal with the consequences of it. And that's *never* funny. People in the backwash of a sensual lifestyle don't come to me and my staff to talk about the lasting joys of illicit sex. They wonder about their family; or what they should do about this disease; or how they can deal with this incestuous relationship that is tearing the home apart; or what the couple should do with information that's going to break their parents' hearts now that she's pregnant out of wedlock.

It would be bad enough if it were limited to the world, but, as I mentioned in my introduction, it is now in the Church—the place most people would consider to be the ultimate bastion of holiness.

The Truth: God's Timeless Counsel for Christians

I am grateful that God talks straight when it comes to moral purity. I'm grateful He doesn't stutter or shuffle or shift His position. I'm even more grateful that He doesn't laugh. It's as if He is looking His people directly in the eye and lovingly yet firmly saying, "I want you to hear this very clearly. I'll make it brief and simple." And He then leaves us with a decision regarding personal holiness. Only one decision pleases Him—*obedience.*

As John Brown, a nineteenth-century Scottish theologian, once stated: "H*oliness* does not consist in mystic speculations, enthusiastic fervors, or uncommanded austerities; *it consists in thinking as God thinks and willing as God wills.*"[7]

That's what the Apostle Paul is asking of the reader in chapter 4 of 1 Thessalonians. He got his foot in the door in that last part of chapter 3 when he set forth a foundational guideline on how to *"really live"* as we *"stand firm in the Lord"* (v. 8). And what does that include?

> *And may the Lord cause you to increase and abound in love for one another, and for all men, just as we also do for you; so that He may establish your hearts unblamable in holiness.* (vv. 12–13a)

What a great way to live—*"unblamable in holiness"!* Confident living is directly linked to being *"unblamable."* It's better than knowing the answers to all the questions on a test, or having plenty of money, or earning an advanced degree. There's no security like being free of blame. When we are established in holiness, living unblamable lives of moral purity, we can smile at life. We can take its pressures and enjoy its pleasures. And then when marriage comes along, we can enjoy the partnership of the opposite sex, including all the joys of sexual delights.

Make no mistake about it, God is pleased when married partners enjoy a healthy sex life in marriage. He applauds it. And why shouldn't He? He invented it. His Word clearly states that marriage is to be held in honor and that the marriage bed is to be undefiled—free of blame (Heb. 13:4). But the implied warning is clear: If we remove sex from its original, God-given context, it becomes *"sexual immorality," "lustful passion,"* and *"impurity."*

In Your Walk, Excel!

1 Thessalonians 4:1–2

Finally then, brethren, we request and exhort you in the Lord Jesus, that, as you received from us instruction as to how you ought to walk and please God (just as you actually do walk), that you may excel still more. (v. 1)

We have other ways of saying "excel" today: "Go for it. Give it your best shot. Don't just drift; pursue!" Or, as many parents often say, "Get with it!" Paul says, in effect, "Just as we have written you and have served as models before you, I encourage you to excel in your walk. *Get with it!* Make something happen in your life. Don't just drift along in a fog of mediocrity. Go the second mile. Excel!"

If you're a C student, try your best for a B. If you tend to be rather laid back in life, now is the time to go beyond your normal level. I exhort you to give yourself to diligence. Overcome that tendency toward laziness. All of that and more is involved in excelling.

While advocating an excelling lifestyle, Paul zooms in on one specific area that needs constant attention: moral purity.

In Your Morals, Abstain!

1 Thessalonians 4:3–6

For this is the will of God, your sanctification; that is, that you abstain from sexual immorality. (v. 3)

He has written strong and emotional words regarding our spiritual walk. We are to excel in it. Now he specifies our moral life. Whoever wishes to excel in his or her spiritual walk must come to terms with an inner battle: sexual lust. Yes, it's a battle . . . a vicious, powerful, relentless fight that won't suddenly stop when we turn fifty. And it won't end just because we may lose our mate. Nor will it decrease because our geography changes, or because we are well educated, or because we may be isolated behind prison walls, or because we remain single, or even because we enter the ministry. The struggle to be morally pure is one of those issues from which no one is immune. That includes *you!* Now let's understand what God is saying here.

"This is the will of God." Very seldom will you find such straight talk in Scripture. When it comes to remaining morally pure, you don't need to pray and ask whether it is God's will. *"This* is *the will of God . . . abstain from sexual immorality."* That last word is translated from the Greek word *porneia.* Obviously, we get our words *pornography* or *pornographic* from that original term. It refers to any kind of intimate, sexual encounter apart from one's marital partner. It would include, of course, intimate encounters with the opposite sex or with the same sex. Fornication, adultery, or homosexuality would be included in *porneia.* Clearly, the command is that we are to *"abstain."* Abstain means exactly that: *abstain.* Outside marriage, have nothing to do with sexual involvements with others.

Now in the fog of horizontal standards, you will be left with any number of options. You will be told by some to be discreet, but certainly not abstain. "I mean, let's don't be fanatical about this." A few may even counsel you, "It would be dangerous for you to play around with somebody else's mate, so don't do that. And, for sure, you need to watch out for disease." But wait. Abstain, in Scripture, doesn't simply mean "watch out" or "be discreet." It means have *nothing* to do with something. Others' advice continues: "It's unwise for you to cohabit with a partner in your family. That's incest." It is not only unhealthy, but it is illegal. "If you're a teacher, you shouldn't be intimate with your students. That's not professionally wise, so don't do that," some would caution. But again I remind you: Scripture clearly states that it is God's will that we abstain. Moral purity is a matter of abstaining, not simply being careful.

How relieving it is to know exactly where we stand with our holy God! Now then, let's be very specific: If you are not married, there are no sexual exceptions provided for you. It is the will of God that you not be sexually intimate with any other person until marriage. That's what Scripture teaches both here and elsewhere. That is how to walk in obedience. It is God's best. Furthermore, it is for our good and it enhances God's glory.

I am pleased to add that we are not left with simply a stark command. Amplifying counsel follows in verses 4 and 5:

> *That each of you know how to possess his own vessel in sanctification and honor, not in lustful passion, like the Gentiles who do not know God.*

It is God's will that we abstain from moral impurity. It is *also* His will that we know how to do that. I suggest that you must become a student of *yourself* in order to know how to handle your battle with sexual lust. Those who fail to know themselves will lose the battle and ultimately become enslaved to lust. In order for one to *"possess his own vessel,"* there must be a practical, working knowledge of one's own tendencies.

You know what kind of student you are, academically, in order to pass the course. You have to apply what you know will work in order to pass the test, and accomplish the course, and get the degree or the diploma, correct? In the realm of your intimate life, there must be another equally diligent application of knowledge. Each of us is to know how to *"possess his own vessel"*—meaning, maintain purity in one's own body.

The point? In order to abstain from *porneia,* we must become alert and disciplined students of our bodies; how they function, what appeals to them, and what weakens as well as strengthens them. We are to know how to control our inner drive, how to gain mastery over it, and how to sustain ourselves in a life of purity rather than yielding to lustful passions.

Let me amplify that by putting it in practical words no one can possibly misunderstand. Within the media there are certain things that you and I cannot handle. We are to know ourselves well enough to admit that and to face the fact that certain sensual stimuli weaken us. We simply cannot tolerate those things and stay pure. The obvious conclusion is this: We are wrong to traffic in them. There are certain films and pictures in magazines that you and I cannot handle. There are certain television programs and late-night channels we have no business watching. There are certain people who, by their stimulating conversation, weaken us. There are settings too tempting, touches too personal, and liberties that are too much for us to handle. We are fools to play around with them. They create appealing temptations we simply cannot control. So if we are committed to abstain, we stay clear of them.

Such decisions are difficult to make and even more difficult to implement, but it is all part of our knowing how to *"possess [our vessels] in sanctification and honor."* Remember this: No one automatically remains morally pure. Abstention from sexual immorality is never an easy-come, easy-go issue. As I said earlier, it's a battle. We're talking *warfare!*

The battle rages in the realm of certain activities that are sexually stimulating. Even certain parties, places, kinds of music, and seductive pastimes can weaken us. Again, we are fools to tolerate those things. A person who is trying to recover from alcoholism realizes he is fighting a losing battle if he chooses to live on the second floor above a bar. No question about it, it will lead to failure. There is more:

> *And that no man transgress and defraud his brother in the matter because the Lord is the avenger in all these things, just as we also told you before and solemnly warned you.* (v. 6)

Some would get around total sexual abstention by saying, "Well, what we could do is just keep this within the family. It's okay if it's between two family members or among Christians." But He corners us here as well. He adds that *"no [one] transgress and defraud his brother in the matter, because the Lord is the avenger in all these things."*

This verse refers not only to members in the family of God but to individual family members—the indecent practices of relating intimately to one's daughter or daughter-in-law, son or son-in-law, mother, stepmother, father, stepfather, and on and on, covering the whole realm of incest. Such indecent, unlawful acts defraud our family members!

Now to state it painfully straight, God clearly and unequivocally stands against extramarital sex, homosexual sex, and sexual encounters with individuals outside of marriage under ANY situation. I repeat, the command is direct and dogmatic: *"Abstain from sexual immorality."*

As I write this, I realize I am not the only one saying these things. But I confess, sometimes I feel like a lonely voice in our day. And because some illustrations could appear as gossip, I choose not to use anyone else but myself as an example. Allow me to tell you *my* story.

My wife and I were married in June of 1955. We both were quite young. I finished my schooling and then faced the need to fulfill my military obligation. Back in the 1950s the military was not an option to choose but a requirement to be fulfilled. Because their time requirement best suited my particular situation, I chose the Marine Corps . . . an outfit not known for its moral purity.

I received the promise from my recruiting officer that if I joined, I would not have to serve my military duty overseas. And since I was married, that certainly was appealing to me;

because I was enjoying life with my bride and the last thing we wanted was a forced separation from each other. I really wanted to be with her. But, through a chain of events too lengthy to explain, I wound up eight thousand miles from home. Stationed in the Orient for over a year, I was suddenly faced with sexual temptation as I had never known it.

Before I ever dropped the seabag off my shoulder on the island of Okinawa, I was faced with a tough decision. I was going to make my home in a barrack that was characterized by a godless lifestyle. Venereal disease was not uncommon among those on the island. Living with a woman in the village was as common as breathing smog in Southern California. If you lived in Okinawa, you slept around. And it wasn't uncommon for the chaplain who was supposed to lecture incoming marines about purity to ultimately joke his way through and tell you where to go to get penicillin shots. Welcome to the real world, Swindoll.

I realized, especially since I had known the joys of intimacy in marriage, that temptation would be incredibly strong. Surrounded by men who couldn't have cared less about the things of God, away from my home and free from physical accountability to my wife and my family, I would soon become another nameless marine on the back streets of Okinawan villages. But I was a Christian. I determined then and there to "*abstain from sexual immorality.*" How I praise my Lord for His sustaining strength!

By the grace of God, the decision that I made back in the late 1950s allows me to speak and write today with confidence. Had I not been preserved from unfaithfulness, I would have to pass rather hurriedly and embarrassingly over this passage and similar sections of Scripture. I sincerely doubt that I would have pursued the ministry had I fallen into sexual lust.

Candidly, I had to be tough on myself. There were times when I had to be downright *brutal* with my emotions. I had to make some tough, spartan decisions . . . unpopular decisions among a bunch of guys who tried everything in the book to tempt me. I was determined to be different so that I could reach those fellow marines with a message that had integrity. Let me clarify something, lest you misunderstand. God showed me it wasn't my job to clean up the goldfish bowl; it was my job to fish. I wasn't called to lead a flag-waving crusade for moral purity across the Orient. It was my job to live clean whether anybody else did or not. To put it bluntly, I was not to put my hands on someone who wasn't my wife. I wasn't even to *talk* about such things. Today I can speak from experience when I write these words: Sexual abstention works. It pays rich and rewarding dividends. It works . . . even in the life of a young, red-blooded marine surrounded by endless opportunities to yield.

And God made it clear to me that if I would abstain from sexual immorality, He would honor that. And His Spirit came to my rescue time and again. I had no corner on strength. I was often in the path of temptation, as anyone reading these words right now would understand, but I refused to surrender. Those were lonely days away from home for almost eighteen months. I was often burning with desire for my wife. But, thank God, I was committed to abstaining from immorality.

How did I make it? I involved myself in things that were wholesome, things that paid off, things that kept me busy, active, and fulfilled. I cultivated my musical abilities by becoming much more proficient in several instruments. I also was involved in an aggressive athletic program, spending most of my spare time with men who were committed to the same wholesome objectives. In my mind, the village was "off limits." I didn't even drop in and get a soft drink in the village bars. I couldn't handle it. When I got off the bus that took me to my destination, I looked straight ahead and walked fast. That little island had physically attractive women and over five thousand places of prostitution. I never touched one of them. Obviously, I saw them . . . but I refused to yield.

In my heart I knew that once I broke, once I stepped into that sensual world, I would not stop. I knew the drive that was inside me *couldn't* be stopped once I yielded. And I probably would not even have wanted to. It's like breaking with a diet. Once you take off the restraint, it's much easier to say, "Who cares?" Once you've eaten a little chocolate cake following lunch, that night it's *half a pie!*

Perhaps you are thinking, "That just mocks me, because my lifestyle isn't there. I've compromised sexually . . . I'm not walking in purity." Wait! My message to you isn't complicated—*start today!* It's time to take charge, my Christian friend. Telling yourself it won't work is the very thing that keeps you from a life of moral purity and its rewards. Stop lying to yourself! If you are born from above, if you are a child of God, then this passage is addressed to *you.* Your name belongs at the beginning of these verses.

See verse 1? *"Finally then,* brethren . . ." Put your name there. This is specific instruction for you, child of God. No one else has the power. To be very frank with you, it's beyond me how an unsaved person can stay out of someone else's life. Only by the power of the living Christ and His Spirit can this kind of life be carried out. If you really want to live in moral purity, yet you are not a Christian, then put first things first. You need to come to Christ. Becoming a Christian precedes cleaning up your moral act. Trusting in the Lord Jesus Christ is primary. Only then can you call upon the power you will need to walk in personal holiness.

Even then, I remind you, it won't be easy or automatic. You'll still need to apply the techniques I've mentioned to sustain your commitment to purity. I have found there are times when temptation is so fierce I have to be almost rude to the opposite sex. That may not sound very nice, but that's the price I'm willing to pay. It is worth it, believe me.

Some of you are husbands and fathers. The habits of fidelity you are forming directly affect your wife and children at home. How careful are you with personal holiness? How consistent? How tough are you on yourself? You cannot depend on anyone else to provide you with a moral standard. YOUR moral standard is the one that's going to keep you pure . . . or lead you astray. Isn't it time you became serious about moral purity?

You may be single, attractive, and capable. You may have entered a fine career. That's great . . . but it is also possible that you have begun to compromise your morals. You may find yourself saying, "It feels so good, and I am so lonely, and it is so accessible, so secret." Wait . . . it *isn't* secret! There is no "secret sin" before God. Furthermore, it won't remain a secret on earth forever.

See what it says in verse 6? It's not often that the Lord calls Himself an *Avenger,* but He does in this case. The meaning? "One who satisfies justice by punishing or disciplining the wrongdoer." Not all of that avenging will wait until the judgment day. Some of it happens now in the form of anxiety, conflict, guilt, disease, insanity . . . even death.

By the way, 1 Corinthians 6:18 is a pretty significant verse. In a context much like the one we've been considering, the writer exhorts the reader not to compromise morally. The verse says:

> *Flee immorality. Every other sin that a man commits is outside the body, but the immoral man sins against his own body.*

Practically speaking, all other sins can be fairly well managed in an objective manner. But this one comes in on you. In today's terms, it's an "inside job." In many ways, sexual sins take a personal toll on the victim, leaving the person in bondage, increasingly less satisfied, and on a downward spiral which only results in greater tragedy.

Few have ever said it better than Evangelist Billy Graham:

In every area of our social life we see

operating the inevitable law of diminishing returns in our obsession with sex. Many do something for a thrill only to find the next time that they must increase the dose to produce the same thrill. As the kick wears off, they are driven to look for new means, for different experiences to produce a comparable kick. The sex glutton is tormented by feelings of guilt and remorse. His mode of living is saturated with intense strain, unnatural emotions, and inner conflicts. His personality is thwarted in its search for development. His passions are out of control, and the end result is frustration. In his defiance of God's law and society's norm, he puts a death-dealing tension on his soul. His search for new thrills, for new kicks, for exciting experiences keeps him in the grip of fear, insecurity, doubt, and futility. Dr. Sorokin says: "The weakened physical, emotional, and spiritual condition of the sex glutton usually makes him incapable of resisting the accompanying pressures, and he eventually cracks under their weight. He often ends by becoming a psychoneurotic or a suicide."[8]

When just a small boy, I remember memorizing the following:

Sow a thought, and you reap an act;
Sow an act, and you reap a habit;
Sow a habit, and you reap a character;
Sow a character, and you reap
a destiny.

How true! And we never come to the place where we can call a halt to the sowing-reaping process.

I heard of a Christian leader who interviewed a veteran missionary who was then in his eighties. The interviewer asked, "Tell me, when did you get beyond the problem with lust?" In candor the godly gentleman answered, "It hasn't happened yet. The battle still goes on!" If you're waiting to outgrow the battle, don't hold your breath.

In Your Reasoning, Remember!

1 Thessalonians 4:7–8

For God has not called us for the purpose of impurity, but in sanctification. (v. 7)

Paul uses *"sanctification"* for the third time in this passage. It's a theological term referring to our pilgrimage, our progress from earth to heaven. Perhaps we could call it our growth pattern.

Remember this: You and I have been called to operate in the sphere of spiritual progress. God has called us to be in a spiritual growth pattern. Sometimes we're up . . . sometimes down. Sometimes we're more victorious than other times. But the progress is a movement forward and higher. God certainly has *not* called us for the purpose of impurity, even though we continue to live in a world socked in by a moral fog.

Consequently, he who rejects this is not rejecting man but the God who gives His Holy Spirit to you. (v. 8)

The second thing to remember is: To reject a lifestyle of holiness is to reject the God who empowers you to live it. Holy living is inseparably linked to believing in a holy God.

The Choice: A Decision Only You Can Make

Let me conclude my thoughts in this booklet by simplifying your options. Actually, you have two. First, you can choose to live your life in a horizontal fog. If that is your choice, the results are predictable. You will continue to drift in a fog of moral uncertainties. Your disobedience will result in a series of rationalizations that will leave you empty. Guilt and grief will be your companions. You can choose to live like that. If you do, you open up a door of misery for yourself. You'll play at church. You'll toss around a few religious words. But before very long your lifestyle will match the atmosphere around you. Your eyes will no longer tear up. Your conscience will no longer sting. Your heart won't beat faster. You may even stop blushing. A jaded, horizontal lifestyle is an option. But it has those consequences . . . those terrible consequences.

Why? The Avenger. God doesn't let His children play in the traffic without getting hurt. Your disobedience will result in increasing personal misery.

Second, you can choose to live your life vertically on target. The benefits? You will honor the God of moral absolutes. And your obedience will result in greater personal confidence and habits of holiness. It will begin to come supernaturally. You'll find yourself stronger, more secure, possessing a healthy self-image.

Internally, we're a little like an automobile. The God who made us built us with all the right lights on our internal dashboard. I don't know of anybody who after purchasing a new car also buys a little hammer for the glove compartment. Let's imagine a weird scene. Let's say that as two men are driving along, one of the lights on the dashboard starts flashing red. The one says to his friend, "Hand me that hammer in the glove compartment, okay? Thanks." Tap . . . Tap . . . Bamm . . . Bamm . . . Pow! "There! Now we've gotten rid of *that* light." Smoke is coming out of the hood, yet the guy keeps driving along.

How foolish! And yet, it isn't difficult to find people who will hand out hammers. As they do, they say, "Aw, that's needless guilt. We're in an age where guilt is no longer considered important. You need to get rid of all that stuff." But wait . . . that's NECESSARY guilt! God help us when we don't have it! It's the conscience that bites into us deep within and stings us when we compromise our moral purity. When we sin, it's *supposed* to hurt. We are *supposed* to be miserable when we compromise morally. That's the red light flashing down inside. It's God's way of saying, "Pull over . . . stop. Lift the hood. Deal with the real problem."

Jonathan Edwards, one of the great preachers of early American history, once made this resolution: "*Resolved,* Never to do any thing, which I should be afraid to do if it were the last hour of my life."[9]

You have available to you the power that's necessary to solve the real problems of your life. He is Jesus Christ. And once you have the Savior, you also have the Holy Spirit. He will come inside not to mock you but to help you; not simply to cry with you over how strong the temptation is but to empower you to overcome it. You can do all things through Him who keeps on pouring His power into you. Even if you have never done it in your life, you can begin a life of power today. There's no checklist. There's no probation period. There's no long list of responsibilities that you must fulfill before God will give you the power. If you've never met the Savior, holiness begins at the cross, where Christ paid the penalty for sin. Take Him now.

Holy Father in Heaven: Our world is a difficult one in which to live. The fog is thick and the heat is stifling. It's difficult . . . but not impossible. Thankfully, Your power provides us with hope . . . hope to start anew, even though we have failed; hope to press on, even though we are afraid; hope to walk in moral purity, even though we are weak.

I pray for all who have picked up and read this booklet. I pray that You would use it to turn their hearts toward You . . . to help them break the syndrome of immorality, to find true freedom, happiness, and holiness by hearing Your Word, obeying Your counsel, and walking in Your truth. In the invincible name of Jesus Christ, Amen.

[1]John White, *The Fight* (Downers Grove: InterVarsity Press, 1976), p. 179.

[2]Charles W. Colson, *Loving God* (Grand Rapids: Zondervan Publishing House, 1983), p. 131.

[3]Kyle Yates, *Preaching from the Prophets* (North Nashville: Broadman Press, 1953), p. 152.

[4]Karl Menninger, *Whatever Became of Sin?* (New York: Bantam Books, Inc., 1978), p. 138.

[5]Jerry White, *Honesty, Morality, and Conscience* (Colorado Springs: NavPress, 1979), p. 184.

[6]Billy Graham, *World Aflame* (New York: Doubleday & Co., Inc., 1965), pp. 21–22.

[7]John Brown, *Expository Discourses on 1 Peter* (Edinburgh: Banner of Truth Trust, reprint edition, 1848), 1:106. Italics in original.

[8]Billy Graham, *World Aflame* (New York: Doubleday & Co., Inc., 1965), p. 23.

[9]Jonathan Edwards, *The Works of Jonathan Edwards,* 2 vols., revised and corrected by Edward Hickman (Carlisle: The Banner of Truth Trust, reprint edition, 1976), 1:XX. Italics in original.

Other Booklets by Charles R. Swindoll

The following **Vital Issues Booklets** have been written by Charles R. Swindoll, published by Multnomah Press, and are available in most Christian bookstores as well as through Insight for Living:

Anger
Commitment
Demonism
Destiny
Divorce
Eternal Security
God's Will
Hope
Integrity
Leisure
Sensuality
Singleness
Stress
Tongues
Woman

Additional booklets by Charles R. Swindoll, ***Attitudes, Impossibilities, The Lonely Whine of the Top Dog, Peace . . . in Spite of Panic,*** and ***Prayer,*** have been published by Insight for Living and may be purchased from their offices. These booklets are not available in local Christian bookstores.

Many Christian bookstores do carry Charles R. Swindoll's most recent booklets, ***When Your Comfort Zone Gets the Squeeze*** as well as ***Moral Purity.*** Both titles have been published by Insight for Living and distributed by Multnomah Press.